CHANGE YOUR THINKING

CHANGE
YOUR THINKING

ANDRÉ DAIGLE

[Change tes pensées, translated from French by
Pacita Consuelo L Maaliw]

Change Your Thinking
[Change tes pensées, translated from French by Pacita Consuelo L Maaliw]
Copyright © 2015 by Editions Dedicaces LLC
All rights reserved. No part of this book may be used or reproduced in any form whatsoever without written permission except in the case of brief quotations embodied in critical articles or reviews.
Published by:
  Editions Dedicaces LLC
  12759 NE Whitaker Way, Suite D833
  Portland, Oregon, 97230
  www.dedicaces.us
Library of Congress Cataloging-in-Publication Data
Daigle, André
  Change your Thinking, by André Daigle.
  p. cm.
  ISBN-13: 978-1-77076-520-7 (alk. paper)
  ISBN-10: 1-77076-520-4 (alk. paper)
If you're constantly struggling with health,
while others live a lot of luck and health, well ...

You too can attract luck and health; you have only to draw the power of positivity in your life! Americans call it

'Positive Thinking'!

Buddha himself said that all we are is the result of what we think of.

Psychologist William James also admitted that the greatest discovery of our generation is to realize that the human being can change his life by changing his way of thinking.

Born to a humble family, he managed nonetheless to pursue his university studies in Educational Sciences, in Literature and in Psychology. After twelve years of educating young people, he will then choose to get involved with adults who were in search of motivation and wished to improve their lives – which he did for 30 years!

Now retired, he shares with us a positive way of thinking; he invites us to put it into constant practice, if we wish to overcome the struggles of everyday life, and attract its many gifts of life, such as luck and health!

Hence this little book, aimed at inspiring confidence in all of us; even in those who find themselves unmotivated, anxious, and stuck with to the daily gloom.

Through a short biography, the author shows that nearly boring life does not stop anyone from achieving their goals.

He then talks about having a positive attitude, and the importance of self-giving from knowing what you want, and to want it. He thoroughly explains to us the power of thought, the use of mental cinema and autosuggestion. He even makes a nod to the psychosomatic world, to make us understand the strange interdependence between the mind and the body, all in a style halfway between speaker and storyteller.

Finally, to all those who think that living 'is hell!', or those who believe themselves 'born to the failure and to misery, he says, 'Bullshit! It's all in your mind!'

Contents

Preface xi
First Part 1
   Once upon a time 2
   An entire purchase! 6
   Farewell! Cross my heart and hope to… oink! 8
   My young sisters 11
   Friends, let us leave quietly! 15
   Friends! That's it, let's get out of here! 17
   Friends! Leave quietly! Still? We'll definitely have to keep up! 19
   Could I fancy you some coincidences? 24
   Thunderclap! 27
Part Two 29
   What the hell was he doing in my galley? 30
   The atmosphere, the heat! Yeah, right! 33
   We will 'be sponges'! 34
   First important point: 36
      Rather believe than doubt! 36
      It's much easier to doubt than to believe! 37
      Yet … the deuce! 37
   Second important point: 40
      Give your 100% 40
      Little 'asides' 43
   3rd important point: 47
      Quiet confidence 47
      Your car's on the driveway! 47
   4th major and important point: 49

- Confidence!..49
- The Biggest of the World..................................53
- Yeah! But...55
- 5th Important point:..57
  - We are unique!...57
- 6th important point:...59
  - What's your goal?..59
- 7th important point:...63
  - The world all around you?..............................63
- 8th important point:...70
  - The power of thought.....................................70
- 9th important point:...75
  - The main course: Psychosomatic life!............75
  - How does it work?...76
  - A small digression 78
  - Thought vs frame..78
  - Having bad blood!...79
- 10th important point:.......................................82
  - A funny way for thinking?..............................82
  - How does it go?...82
  - Let us choose..86
- Addendum...89
  - Can we be happy alone?.................................90
- Epilogue..93
- Why not a second epilogue?............................95
  - The killer question..97

Preface

Whether we follow every school of thought imaginable – *Knowledge of Self, Personal Growth, Human Relations, Therapies of all kinds* – whether we read all the books of *Positive Thinking* and all the *Secrets,* if we allow ourselves to live by our fears, our doubts, by our unnecessary suffering, we will attract problems, illness, misfortune!

Very many people have experienced, from their infancy, negative approaches to life: '*Don't do that! No touching!*' Later, television and newspapers, have added to this sad situation, showing constantly all of the gloom and miseries of the world. So we shouldn't be surprised to find how it's almost normal for many people, made adults, wanting to generalize and think that *living is appalling.*

We must put a stop to this! I say, that the most ordinary guy, who moreover has met a lot of obstacles in life, is not as damned as we'd make him out to be. Although he was born in a remote village, almost unknown, I am sure that his fate will depend more *on his attitude and his way of thinking.*

That's the short story I want to tell you in the *first part* of this little book. The story of the guy who doesn't ask questions! This is from the guy who faced everything with *quiet confidence.*

Yes, there was gloom in the air. You can cry a lifetime, be justified, accusing everyone, or better, strive to develop a state of trust; which leads us to believe in ourselves, which then leads us to believe in life.

We all meet difficulties, we all live through situations that seem insurmountable, and we all have the choice to feel sorry for ourselves or get out of our miserable chairs once and for all.

When will something beautiful, great, wonderful, happen to us?

The day we believe it; the day we change our old negative software for a new one full of *confidence!* Not the one that makes us parade in front of people, but one that makes us sleep soundly knowing that tomorrow something beautiful is waiting for us!

It's especially with this amazing way of thinking that will be discussed in the *second part* of the book. You will see how this ordinary guy came through, thanks to *Positive Thinking*, practicing an unusual way to see his fate; which enables him even today in his advanced age, still enjoying health, good fortune and all the other gifts of life.

A bit like the Dalai Lama, he was able to contemplate the lotus flower on the surface of the water, not the mud at the bottom of the pond!

First Part

A few anecdotes from the life of the guy next door, who finally made it through. Throughout his life, despite several challenges, he was able to always feel favored.

ONCE UPON A TIME

I had just finished my studies, when the English Jesuits of the esteemed *Loyola College* offered me my first job: to teach for them.

Imagine! A small French Canadian, Quebecois, Francophone – like Elvis Graton said – settled in as a teaching among the very *Irish* English! A young *100% Quebecois*, as would we have said, from the peaceful village of Saint-Marc-sur-Richelieu! At the time, it was called Saint-Marc-sur-*'le'*- Richelieu.

To tell you the truth, as far as we're concerned, we were not quite *on the* Richelieu, since we lived in a *country road*, somewhere between the wood of Saint-Antoine and that of Saint-Amable; which will never be, for sure, a remarkable reference.

However, that fact that I showed my face in an institution of the west of the city, seemed to me to that point, a reason to puff my chest, or to *snap my braces,* in our usual jargon. Understand that in a little more than my adolescence years, I went from the small farm boy in worn *overalls* to a quasi-intellectual in a neat tie! Better yet, if I place myself at the beginning – I would almost say, *at the very beginning of the colony!* That would have brought great pleasure to some of my bully relatives, who envy the wisdom of my age.

So if I place myself at the beginning, the little kid, blue eyes like a cold sky, born of a very sick mother, was far from thinking that one day he would join the court of the great beards of knowledge.

Yes, when I was three years and two months old, my mother was taken away by tuberculosis. She taught a beat up little school, worn and pierced by harsh winds. Her tiny pittance had not allowed her to buy all the necessary logs for firewood. She had caught a cold and then, left this world at a tender age, because she was poorly treated, because she was too poor.

So I went out to with all the philosophy and all the sadness of my age. 'He doesn't understand,' said aunt Lucienne. Yet I understood everything. I also understood why later, my father was crying so often. Sometimes secretly, sometimes surprised, *'saying that his ring hurt him!'*

Seeing how the farm was in decline, it was obvious he was in pain. Even the mountains of empty cans behind the dilapidated house shamelessly displayed his discouragement.

Yet around, life was almost cherished by the people of the effaced area, where electricity wasn't yet operational. *'Estris'ty'* used to say Uncle Peter. Indeed, we warmed ourselves with wet birch, *used coal fuel* for lighting, and too often we ate *salted lard*.

'Hey guys! Pick up your things!'

That was how we learned, my brother and I, that we had to go live some time with our grandparents in their old ancestral home, surrounded by orchards, vineyards and the old game of croquet.

Croquet! The extraordinary place where the Sunday's *belle visite* came to show us their city-folk skills! There was also the stream where we fished for minnows, for lack of large fish. Not to mention the old car bodies all *defunct* and dilapidated behind the aging shed.

Uncle François studied mechanics and gathered all he could find in the area. I don't know if he was able to build a car with all the old junk, but I remember our cousins from the city used the roof of one of these old cars as a sunbathing spot.

Those were our first stronghold against the girls of our age. Although Jeannine, our young neighbor next door, could introduce us to something too; but her parents were too alert.

The life near the forest brought us to dream about wolves. All night they ran in a frenzied manner in the corridor between the staircase and the attic. Some rose up and became *werewolves* or *lynxes*, who, with big knives slaughtered us, each one in turn, my brother and I. Somewhat in the same manner as my uncle and aunts do when they *slaughtered* a pig to replenish the *salting tub*.

Grandma also did the same with her hens. Such images gave us nightmares each time we ate to our fill.

Since, we're speaking about animals, let me talk about our good *Prince*. He was a dog that was over 100 years old in dog years, who lead *a dying life with no end*, as might have said   Jean de Lafontaine, or Shakespeare.

Nevertheless, Uncle François resigned himself to draw him into the barn and to knock him out, just to end his suffering. After a few hits with a sledgehammer, it was not very pretty. I speak of course of the dog;

though the uncle *did not seem so well* either, as a result of his act of mercy.

There was also that damn rooster. And I had so much faith in my grandmother Tanguay!

One day she sent me to the neighbor, reassuring me that this package of feathers that paced the slope was not at all bad. I haven't lost faith in her, since she was able to explain to me why the fool rooster jumped on me anyway.

'It doesn't hurt! It doesn't hurt!'

My grandmother did not know Yvon Deschamps, but she knew how to philosophize anyway, sometimes.

My arms were branded for a long time! Fortunately, a little later, we had measles, my brother and I. I say fortunately, because, thanks to the many additional red marks, I did not have to explain my quite painful collapse in the land of *chickens!* Moreover – *another unexpected benefit* – norms required at the time, that we should be kept in the dark for the duration of that contagious disease!

An entire purchase!

My dad ended up remarrying. At the same time, he had found us a mother. She was played with us, was sewed, and made fudge.

'Is there any more?' I dared to ask, stammering as I returned from school one day.

'Forget it! I ate everything!'

She said she had eaten the fudge in secret like a *'safre'*, *a glutton* to *tease* us of course. We used to say *'sarfe'* among us; it made more *safre*, more greedy!

Our first winter together was difficult; everything ran out. We did not even have enough warm clothes to brave the storm and the snow on the way to school. She made us learn in a few months our classes' program worth a year and a half.

The following year, we had real felt boots as our Christmas *bonus*. Mine were of a coffee color, and I laced them high. I have never seen the like in all of *'myyy'* life, as some snobs say. I must add that they came from far away, through mail order; from a popular *catalog* of the time.

Then it was back to school life. The caned life, the *bickering* life, the life of first love, the life of *apple core* exchanges!

One day, one of the cousins decided to leave school. For a few hours only! His father brought him back *illico*, kicking him in the butt during the trek back to school. Poor René! Must say that the Department of Education was not yet created, and the parents had to do violence to themselves, and quickly had to find solutions to the problem of dropping out.

Moreover, that year, we were all almost held back. Indeed, during one night, our school burned down. And also burned our desks, our books, and especially Julia's stick; the one she seemed to use on most of the students' back, to get rid of her frustrations.

'Camille! Come here!'

We all held our breath, knowing that the storm would soon hit; poor Camille. He could not remember *who could have found the city of Quebec*. He should have tried something!

His momentary ignorance earned him a rain of blows. Full of sympathy, the whole class had begun to cry. Bad reflex: Julia raged all the more!

Often corrections were made in duplicate! First at school, then at home. At the time, although we did not have electricity in the rank, we had all the same phone. Yep! So that even before the child arrived home, parents were already awaiting a sequel of spankings!

Even Leonard made life difficult for us.

'Lucienne!'

He was our age; he was, however, in familiar terms with her. She was actually his cousin.

'Did you see what a kid did at recess? He tore his snowsuit while sliding!'

The kid, was my brother! He then had to wipe a correction more!

'What a great pain in the ass, that Leonard!'

FAREWELL! CROSS MY HEART AND HOPE TO… OINK!

'The father' and 'the mother', as we called them in those days, eventually tired of their miserable lives, sold the property. It was not very common at that time. Farms rather constituted a kind of family wealth that was bequeathed to future generations.

To say that I might have been able to become a seasoned farmer; as long as my brother had sold me his birthright!

So we left for Montreal, *the big village*.

The first time we heard a tram hit the brakes, we were surprised; terribly even, my brother and I!

'*What's that?*' he cried!

'It must be someone who's emptying a sack of grain on the ground,' I said, all radiant.

The noise had stirred the air as it blew from the cylinder, and I really believed my explanation. *You can take a guy out of the country, but it's not always easy to get the country out of a guy!* I think I heard that somewhere!

East Montreal isn't the corner of the earth where the air is the purest! Like plants, humans breathe the smell of refineries; they are often greenish … like plants!

Despite all this, it was still in the corner of the Island, that Richard Séguin, one of our committed singers, found the inspiration to immortalize these refineries with his song *Sous les Cheminées*. If Richard Séguin found inspiration, my brother, took the opportunity to find a mate; in fact, he married one of singer's cousins! There are coincidences in life!

It was also in this same corner of the island, that Patrick Labbé and Mitsou 'coyote'ed'!

I refer, of course, to the movie *Coyote* shot in the country of my adolescence by those two well-known actors.

At Larry Beausoleil's, even! It was that small restaurant where I was introduced to my first part-time job as a waiter, at the corner of our own 'Broadway'.

Larry, it was a carbon copy of the French actor *Gérard Darmon*. You know the one who played *Onassis* on television? The one who had gone in search of *Aznavour* for hours in the film *Emmène-moi* ! Same eyes, same allure.

In the following year, my passion for work had been taken to Mister Baril; 'le *bonhomme* Baril,' as the young ones used to call him. He had at that time, two restaurants – *later three* – that had quick service. First I began by putting on his famous *Broadway Chip*, where Sunday afternoons, I also had to serve the enthusiasts of turf racing, who had *dashingly* returned from Richelieu; the region's racetrack.

At the *Chalet*, his other eatery at the corner of 2e Avenue, we had launched for the first time, *soft ice cream* and *Orange Julep* juice! At least that was new in the area. But despite such beautiful discoveries, it was especially the little bear we had tamed at the door, which brought people in all summer long. People came to see him, but sometimes forgot to buy!

Finally, *'my Boss'* put up a small trailer selling fries, on main street, in Charlemagne, near the bridge. Not far from the family home of Celine Dion, our international star!

Alas! Despite all everyone's enthusiasm, and despite my big *'talent'*, the last canteen hasn't really taken quite off. *Celine was not yet born at the time!*

The following year, I had to convert my talents as restaurateur into that of a grocer. In fact, it became advantageous as my older brother took me to work at *Chez Thisdale*, a placed he managed.

Well! With all this talk of restaurants and groceries, I am, too far away in time. Let's go a few years back.

MY YOUNG SISTERS…

At the time, we had a little sister who grew very quickly. In five or six years, I beckoned her to the roof of the shed for her to slide with me, and dive head first, a few meters down in the neatly piled snow banks along the alley.

I understand better now why she was trying to improvise some kind of *sign of the cross* before every tumble.

Yep! She knew how to pray! We also recited the family rosary to the sound of the voice of the famous Cardinal Léger. I liked to imitate him. '*Ha-ai-l Mary, full of gra-a-ce…*'

Two other little sisters were born afterwards. I spent a few summers taking them around in a kind of buggy, *pram* style of yesteryear. I even taught the youngest to whistle very early in life!

Before settling in the east of the city, we had lived for some time with Aunt Yvonne in Saint-Léonard. Saint-Léonard-de-Port-Maurice, it was called. Her daughter, Thérèse, really knew how to run the *house* and her parents at the same time. What authority!

In fact, when one of them approached her hiding place, she shouted at them.

'*Buzz off!*'

'I'll make you buzz something else,' thundered her father!

And an endless pursuit began; around the table, sometimes at the stairs. This lasted until uncle Clément could take no more.

Nothing's left of that corner of the countryside, just north of the refineries. Since then, the tranquil setting of the time has changed. A highway that we called the 40 was even built. The scenery was still beautiful at the time. Next, at Bérangère Pépin's, our kind teacher, one saw two beautiful rows of young mountain ash or maybe was it ash? Later those trees were cut, and factories were built.

It was *the countryside* and *the city* at the same time; especially the countryside. To remember, I only have to think of frantic early morning race, from the top of the stairs to the outhouse!

There was also a well in the yard that supplied water to the animals in the barn, about ten paces from the old house, that the farmers of the time, the *Robins*, had rented to my aunt first, then to my parents afterwards. The Robins had built a new one not too far from the road.

A cousin of the same family later became my brother-in-law; he just married my sister who had learned to whistle so well.

We also experienced the time when the grocer came to us take *the order*, then returned to deliver. That time on Saturdays, some fifteen children of the row were being lead to the Roussin College in Pointe-aux-Trembles, for a *small glimpse* of the outdoors view, warm weather permitting. We were in the same box of the truck that was used to deliver the week's hops at the breweries. All this was *intoxicating*! In both ways!

I don't remember movies like it. I especially remember the little Suzanne, right next to me, who smelled of hay or of her mother's soap. To say that at school, we chatted all the time, her and I. The *teacher* always told us she would make us kiss if we didn't stop! This professor really disappointed me because she hadn't kept her promise. And I never saw Suzanne with the big black braids ever again.

When we left Saint-Léonard, to live in East Montreal, my parents decided to leave the dog at the *Robins'* farm; why complicate things? When we returned to see him two weeks later, he had died of grief under the gallery; he too did not want to complicate things.

At the school in the city, there were many students and above all, the good *Brothers of Saint Gabriel!* It was very different from provincial classes. I think especially of the headmaster, who was walking with *his ruler* in order to intimidate us. He wasn't successful all the time. Some students' cheap shots continued to flow.

My brother and I, we went to church early in the morning to *serve Mass*. We would collect cigarette butts on our way, then tried to smoke them in secret during the day in the washrooms of the Alfred-Richard school. I remember very well my first puffs of smoke as well as my first official and public reprimands.

You went to the bathroom to smoke? Said my professor, sniffing my hands! Even so, I had taken good care to wash them!

'Smoke? What is that?'

I was trying to be clever!

It was nothing, however, if I compare my situation to that of a friend, who he was condemned by his father, *pumping* cigar after he had picked up, and until that he became green and sick! Ah! The good pedagogy applied in this beautiful time!

One day, a cousin of the family, a priest and a cleric of Saint Viator, stopped *by our place*. We loved his nicknamed, *the small pump* because he knew how to pressure young people, from parish to parish, just to draw them into the college to become religious priests. He had an eye on our vocations, my brother and I. He was even willing to help us financially; an asset for us, who wanted to do advance studies – an advantage for our parents who were not so fortunate.

Friends, let us leave quietly!

We left for the Collège Bourget, at the foot of the shrine of Our Lady of Lourdes, which in turn was clinging to Mount Rigaud, where lies the remain of the legendary *Champ des guérets*. It was not very far away from the Ottawa River, we crossed over with pleasure in the month of June when we were picnicking at Oka, at our buddy Guilbault's. We called him *Wabo*, for the reasons you might just think of! The boy from an Amerindian village agreed to be compared to the real *Wabo*, one of the famous characters of the radio novel, *Séraphin, or Un homme et son péché'* that people were following every day, as religiously as a *family praying the rosary*!

Uncle Elzéar, mayor of our hometown, deplored the lack of priests among our relatives.

'Perhaps, one day, someone will finally decide to lift the family up,' he liked to say.

Alas! The poor man was disappointed!

Like me, my brother did well with his Latin. But when it came to Greek, he preferred to go home. Note that up until today, I still don't know this language, not much more than he does.

Ancient Greek and Latin are obviously dead languages, because they are no longer spoken. I later understood the deep meaning of this statement, when I had to explain to young students newly enrolled in my Latin class. During my presentation, one of them then took his tongue in one hand, and with the other, mimicking the grave gesture of someone pointing a revolver, tragically shot an imaginary bullet in it! His tongue, of course died in a solid and convincing rattle! There! He got it all!

On the other hand, I too had understood something; I understood that the Department allowed much younger students to undertake studies as serious as those of ancient civilizations.

In college, I studied, sometimes drank altar wine – *in secret of course* – ate the apples of the good Father *Racan*, teased the waitresses in the kitchen and skipped my college sometime with the boys of the village, Louis and Richard who unfortunately did not have younger sisters to introduce us to.

I dare not talk too much about the filthy things that have been done within the walls of this renowned college. As we are never alone in such events, talk could tarnish the memory of my learned colleagues of my *Alma Mater* who are today judges, dentists and opera singers.

Friends! That's it, let's get out of here!

One day, both Jacques and I decided, right in the middle of philosophy class, to go and rebuild the world. We did not know yet if we were going to join the well known *Father Pierre, in France*, or at least build a foundation.

The dream *messed up* very quickly.

My buddies turned back while I went along on the North Shore with the *Bersimis* Indians. Previously, I had been picking potatoes at the Ouellettes' at *Grand-Sault*, which was once called the Grand Falls!

We will all, one day or the other, pick potatoes, somewhere in New Brunswick to pay for a journey to the *Terre de Caïn*, or go whale watching; in this region of the world, whales are called 'balèèènes'.

'Hey! You like potatoes, my friend?' (You will recognize here the stupid humor of our famous Têtes à Claques!)

It was the time when some Country artists like Roger Miron, sang: '*À qui le p'tit coeur après neuf heures?*' Meaning 'To whom this little heart belongs, after 9?' In the language of the Indians, it sounded like, '*Win Oté ti pistil Nappi négouïne? Ti ta mé? Ta ti té?...*' Not bad as poetry, isn't it?

The night of the show, I met a girl from the village of *Saint-Louis-du-Ha! Ha!* – not a very funny village, despite its name, since the parents of the girl with whom I had exchanged a few smiles, never wanted me to see her again.

I worked with the installation of a dam on the *Bersimis* river. I also learned a lot about the costs of a project. Some large sub-contractors were working at the time in *pro rata* to their spending; the head mistress of the project company, reimbursed a certain percentage to them.

Therefore! What one has used and worn, excavators, trucks, compressors; to lose sight of them completely! That is to wear them out!

I refer to the gossips that claimed that often the heavy equipment were thrown into the ravines and buried later, to better drive up costs ... *Come on!*

This journey amidst the workers had brought me some money. It had also given me the desire to continue my studies.

Friends! Leave quietly!
Still? We'll definitely have to keep up!

I walked around college by making offers; offers they *could* refuse!

'I have so much money; would you take me as a student resident for two years?'

The *Collège de Saint-Laurent* finally agreed, through the kindness of the director of the time, father Duchesneau. I was able to complete the missing years of philosophy to get my baccalaureate. And at the same time make good on the damned father *Pelo*, the head of the student Pavilion.

One evening there was a card game in big gym, organized to raise the necessary funds for our cultural activities.

We were all excited for the arrival of schoolgirls and interns to help us serve tables. Every schoolboy would have an escort. Luck had it that night I met a brunette, who became *ma blonde*; my girlfriend, if you prefer.

Must say that it's a bit because of my shoelaces, that had delayed me enough, so that some synchronization is done with the little red velvet dress. Yet I would have known that red can be a sign of any danger! But I just saw fire! And at the same time, I forgot Bibiane.

I met Bibiane the summer before, as I worked for the accounting of *Jules d'Alcantara*, the florist. She was little Cécile's friend who knew how to *flirt* with all customers; which did not fail to horrify our chief accountant, an old girl who was surely jealous! I had walked home a few times with Bibiane.

She was a charming girl whom I would have liked to introduce to my parents.

'What? There is no question that you bring me a girl here ... especially a girl I don't know!'

My mother liked to give importance to her responsibilities, liked to control almost everything. She even wanted to choose *our paramours!*

In the fall, Bibiane returned to her boarding school when I returned to my new college.

My studies could have been long and painful – *even shooting* – as said a pub, but luckily, my darling made things rather pleasant, as she came to me often enough, which obviously upset our director.

He watched his students like a hawk. We had to find a corner of the cemetery, including the high stone walls that put us out of sight from his inquisition. And it's there that often our Sunday night rides ended. I remember the old wrought iron bench, paths strewn with flowers, and above all, this calm, mortuary peace!

One day I had to put up a small '*Dusty Western*' type of play. As we played as both male and female roles, I sacrificed myself playing the femme fatale of the saloon, *Lolita*.

My girlfriend lent me clothes and other *fancy accessories*. I never wanted her to wear *them* in the parlor on Sunday in front of my colleagues. Comparing our figures would never have favored me.

I liked the theater. This was not my first experience. Some years before, at the *Bourget*, we put up *Les Fourberies de Scapin*, with the help of our teacher, 'Bydoune', now deceased.

Bydoune – *pronounced Buy-Doon* – was a distortion of the city of *Bytown* as mentioned in the song '*Passant par Bytown... en vidant les bouteilles...*'

Obviously the nickname, strongly alluded to those words! Bydoune liked to empty bottles!

Gerontius' character and *his cursed galley*, gave me a little popularity at the time, and a lot of satisfaction.

'What the hell was he doing in this mess?'

This response came over and over to Scapin, and it still resonates in my mind after all these years.

Our interpretation is likely that Molière will be all crumpled up in his grave to make his sides hurt! Unless it's put him in a rage, and so I expect to meet him in the afterlife with his lantern – *that Diogenes would have lent him, of course!*

Finally, I liked the first college. They told us to enjoy it, it was our best years! There was really something in there. There was little responsibility, a cultured climate, the spirit of family. We engaged in sports, in music. I also saw on the stage of our auditorium lots of artists and international stars: the Companions de la Chanson, the violinist Arthur Leblanc, Félix Leclerc, singers Jean Paul Jeannotte, Pierrette Alarie, and many others!

This is also where I learned to ski. It took all afternoon to climb to the top of the mountain, and a few minutes to come down. We weren't always on our skis. Sometimes we were even hugging some trees when we weren't hugging the monuments of the cemetery, while going *'Down the steep slope!'* A little nod to Roger Lemelin, who wrote *'Down the gentle slope!'*!

My second college in Ville Saint-Laurent, had no major open areas. At most, we had three bowling alleys in the basement and two pool tables on the ground floor. Anyway, what mattered was studying... and meeting girls. Because no one has the right to prepare for his future with just books!

At the university, it's different; we were housed with friends in the *garçonnières*, not far from our classrooms. And, of course, it's easier for our lovers to come to us to prepare our future.

It was an amazing time! I had the privilege to enrich myself in the presence of outstanding faculty, in psychology as much as in the arts. I cannot forget some of my companions and some of my classmates: Renée Claude, Stéphane Venne, Fanfan Dédé ... characters in the art world, beloved of Quebec.

I participated also at this time the famous Theatre Workshop, where a Jean Doat, illustrious French director, came to help us put up the *'Procès à Jésus'* by *Diego Fabbri*, which we had just played at the *Gésu* Theatre! Not related to Jesus you know; even though the room was located inside one of the colleges of the Society of Jesus, the reputed Sainte Marie. This was where I met one of those who teamed with me, Marc Laurendeau, perhaps not *cynical* at the time, but became it so quickly; thanks to his band of the same name. *Les Cyniques* have actually made quite a killing in Quebec in the 60s.

Among the young actors and actresses of my group, I remember Élizabeth Schuvallize, whom we sometimes see on television from time to time. I learned later – *another coincidence* – my wife had gone to *École Saint-Alphonse*, with her, at the end of high school.

COULD I FANCY YOU SOME COINCIDENCES?

I did my studies at Collège *Bourget*; my wife had studied at the École Normale Ignace *Bourget*. Better yet, her parents were married on a beautiful September 14 in 1935! Mine did too! Absolutely *amazing*!

When we got married – *when we made a 'marissage' as would say an old sister-in-law with a very surprising tongue* – I still had a year of study to complete my *degree*, my *Licence*. This degree, in the past, was intended to be what the Master is today.

Luckily my wife had started teaching because scholarships don't arrive as quickly as monthly rent.

What often happens very quickly, however, are children.

So I completed my studies on the roof rack, rocking our first child; even then, we were trying to watch our little TV when the aircraft noise was not too strident above our heads.

To say that today with the closing of Mirabel airport, people from my old corner see again the old problem of the sixties.

There was also a young brother-in-law who came to join us to practice his talent with a pellet gun. Imagine the guy on the other side of the street, who is going to take the bus, saw a madman on the roof of a building, a gun in his hand! Should he ask him if it's a toy, or should he just *get the hell out of there*?

I also have less happy memories.

At night, we had to get up to give our daughter a drink. It was also necessary to make the old worn and misshapen floor creak, that made our downstairs neighbor grumble and grouse.

'If you are not happy, get lost!' I yelled at him one day, with all the confidence of an accomplished show-off!

The poor man probably had a bad heart condition, for he had a severe attack over supper, one day, and disappeared in an ambulance, never to return.

Meanwhile, I accumulated degrees, through grants and loans. At the time, it was necessary to have several *strings to his bow*! This was long before the colorful Jean Marc Chaput spit out this sentence, complete with his Irish curse.

'Have you ever tried to draw the bow with several strings, '*Sacrafice*'!'

But the '*trip*' of the city doesn't last long. It was necessary to expand, have the family growing up, and start to think big: home, leisure, social influence.

At work, we played Latin, ate paella for lunch with Luc and Suzanne. And coincidentally, in the middle of 1967 – the year of the Universal Expo – we had to live a double schedule of work, and had to take advantage of the free afternoon– *what a terrible misfortune!* I could go *poking* around piles of the *Terre des Hommes* pavilions. Of course, then, we had to go scare ourselves in all kinds of rides, with my cousin from Sainte-Adèle, a large rash of small north! Ah! What to become good folk when one is motivated by a hint (!) of pride!

To say that during that time, my wife, through her teaching job, was playing happily in her class, with little devils, thirsty for some desire *to know nothing* of their studies!

One could also become brave when you've spent a few hours at the German cabaret, the *Lowenbräu*, with friends! *Getting a pint* has always been a kind of very safe method to get to achieve a high level of courage! I experienced this karma. It was also the perfect opportunity for me to practice my *hovering* head first down the train for the ride. Today I am wondering about the need to make such somersaults to impress people.

'Sacrebleu! You're all beat up!'

I took in all the thoughts of the people in the family. In fact, two days after my famous *dive*, we were all at the funeral of Grandfather Honorius. My face was hidden behind large sunglasses; what could be interpreted as a sign of deep sympathy on my part to our beloved grandfather. It was mainly to cover up my freshly ravaged face.

THUNDERCLAP!

It's therefore in this state of bliss – *if one puts aside the trivial incident* – a couple friend, suddenly came to disturb our inner calm. This great fool, a dimwitted, miserable – *as said by our grand-son, when he played with the figurines of his pirate ship* – this lout, I say, showed up with his girlfriend in order to surreptitiously plant doubt in my peaceful life!

This *comic* had discovered 'the' truth, the *philosopher's stone*. He took advantage of his enthusiasm to impress me, *to butter me up real good*, like we say.

It's as if he wanted me to ask myself again all the great existential questions that I had already asked. Where am I going? Where do I come from? What of my life?

Personally, I saw myself at the pinnacle of social adventure. In so little time!

We all participate in a range of community movements, experiences as couples, activities in our youth.

We were done for!

And now this intruder was trying to mess up my life, when I had a satisfactory impression that everything went easily; that luck had accompanied me in every part of my daily life. Despite several pitfalls – *I haven't told the whole story yet, of course* – I like the certainty of always being pampered by life. It was my personal way to appreciate things at the time.

ANDRÉ DAIGLE

So why do you want to shake all this up?

Part Two

As promised, in this second part, I will leave out, little by little, personal facts, to arrive at the 'funny' way of thinking, which allowed me to attract more good things from life!

WHAT THE HELL WAS HE DOING IN MY GALLEY?

Our friends had been bewitched. They had an experience in their group that they described as *extraordinary*.

An old man, exceedingly self-taught, gave them the lesson of their lives on *how to live better,* it seemed. Worse, they wanted to *include* my wife and me in their mysterious adventure!

Then I, who had spent more years on the benches of knowledge than on the labor market, I could not allow myself to be *'entangled'* in an adventure sponsored by the *'pseudo-knowledgeable'* kind who were undoubtedly ignorant! Anyway! I had taken courses myself. And indeed, I followed them in big houses of culture! Not in church *basements*, or in corner school gyms!

The way of life can be learned by studying the lives of our ancient authors, of our philosophers, not in groups oh... *pickles*!

How can it be otherwise?

Furthermore, by studying pedagogy, I was taught for a long time, how to *do* and how to *say*. In teaching, it was my turn to tell others what to *do*. I was not going to let any pseudo-philosopher dictate my behavior; because, if I understood it correctly, these famous courses were designed to reform timid people, without collars, the laggards, the fearful, the embarrassed.

I was going forward; the *small* French Canadian was dying in me.

'I don't need this! I'm not embarrassed! I'm able to speak in public! I was even in the theater! Public speaking! I've *seen others*, I have!' I imposed, exasperatedly.

Seen others? I don't know if my subconscious was pushing me to escape that sentence, I, who had just seen '*those*' from Fabiola up close!

Indeed, returning from a teachers' meeting, we stopped at the cabaret of *La Feuille d'Érable*, which, Fabiola, a buxom singer of the time, invited someone to her stage to come and dance the '*twist*' with her. Like a *fool*, I rushed to see her peaks up close. From a distance, they looked like they were on the verge of bursting! Up close, I vividly remember the large blue prominent veins; her bodice was on so tightly.

What I remember most from that evening was my half drunk neighbor, very wise and reflective, came up as he was bent over on his fourth or fifth pint: *glass full, I empty you; empty glass, I pity you!*

'Leave me alone with your *degenerate* kind,' I said with conviction.

'Yes, but, darling...'

My wife was intervening.

In fact, the intruder's *wife*, had spent some school years, with my wife. Friends of my wife became our friends. Until then, I had not suffered; on the contrary, they helped us every so often, especially the time when I was a student, penniless, and without a car. But now they wanted to call into doubt all my years' worth of progress.

'It's not what you think,' they said, 'you might love this!'

Though I know them to be sincere, I could not help but imagine traps!

'You will surely love the atmosphere, the warmth of the group, the humanity!' They insisted.

As I said earlier, I had perhaps not developed a taste for this *human side* of trade in people. Severe education, almost cold, studies in colleges with strict disciplinary requirements, a continual concern for my own self or to negotiate with the entourage, had all gotten me used to play a solitary game.

When someone came home, I always hesitated to go up from the basement to greet him. I was trying to sell myself the idea of being really busy with quite serious things: corrections for assignments, readings of plays, musical works, or very scientific strategies for practice on my pool table!

Referring to their *human warmth* side was probably well placed; but I intended to improve all this... *my way!*

The atmosphere, the heat! Yeah, right!

The Heat could well come from a group of people as different from each other?

I certainly did not want this 'flabbergasted', this dangerous friend, force me to change my way of life; my winning formula.

So much the better, if they were able to discover something new, something wonderful in their group experience.

And then, what? After them, *there was no deluge!*

I certainly did not want start my journey all over again! And at what price this time? Already, this journey was long and arduous. It's great to live through a lot of experiences; but it must end one day, and turn into action.

Although, at this point, I must admit, I was certainly curious about what was going on, in these exalted groups! What was so phenomenal there? How to interpret the fact that even at that time, many people seemed to be strongly attracted by these enigmatic encounters, almost clandestine?

Was it religious sects? Some sort of 'Magical Thinking'? Another *'Secret'*? Like the one written by Rhonda Byrne? Was it promising miraculous means to remake the human race? Or better yet, a simple idiot traps?

To learn more, despite any reluctance that strongly manifested, it was necessary that I come to be convinced to go *at least* see something more closely.

WE WILL 'BE SPONGES'!

I therefore had to live the experience of a *sponge*! You know, the one who wants to *test the waters* first; just going up to the point of making a decision? I therefore let me invite to the last evening of a session of this *'famous'* course.

At the time, experience ended with a public gala. The graduates invited their relatives and friends. They would therefore witness their victories, they said; to take part in their discoveries, their wonder...

With everything that had been told elsewhere, on all these courses in fashion, I was expecting a night of crying, ranting, and an endless exhibition of life issues! This would have been the argument dreamt to flesh out my point of view:

'Could be a case of collective hysteria,' I could've said.

'Just negatives, then.'

However, fortunately, this was not quite what happened. Of course, there were tears, emotions. We saw that some participants were returning from afar, as they say. They had not all the skill required to definitively settle the battle of life in so little time. But, all in all, the exercise was serious.

How to respond to such an experience? Should I believe at the onset to indisputable efficiency? Should I rather question me?   Being puzzled? Doubting?

All this was in fact, a little trigger, staging the first of the important points which I want to talk in this second part of my book; points that will be gradually see the *funn*y way of thinking, proposed at the beginning.

First important point:

Rather believe than doubt!

The gamut of our studies and our intellectual formation of the time sometimes prevented us to have quick faith! Had they not taught us to practice *doubt* during these years of studying philosophy, among others?

Those who had to clear the theories of the time will remember '*I doubt, therefore I am!*' In other words, if you find yourself doing the intellectual approach to self-question, doubting is what makes you an intelligent being who knows how to question; you're a thinking being, an existing being: you're alive!

As for me, the simple act of thinking, 'I think, therefore I am!' Would have been enough to make us realize that we exist! But the great philosophers of past centuries were not always content with such simple things! They *need* to dig further, to question, to doubt.

How will we then, spontaneously, have confidence in life after having practically *deformed* thought?

This doubt or this craving to question, has also heavily rubbed off on our culture, our way of thinking, our education in general. Today, many people are still on the defensive; they always ask all sorts of questions without taking decisions.

There are mostly other reasons explaining why we went to foster *doubt* before *faith*.

IT'S MUCH EASIER TO DOUBT THAN TO BELIEVE!

Have you thought about how complicated it's to believe? For example to believe that something *beautiful, great, wonderful...* could happen to us?

To believe is an extremely difficult thing! You have to be put in an uncomfortable situation; you must force yourself to expect to receive behind the invisible! *What a job!*

However, it's so much easier to doubt! One doesn't have to force himself too long; just think that it should *not* work, it *will not be possible*. That's it!

At that time, we give up just before making the *shade* of an effort.

We are far from the song of Michel Fugain, who said: 'Do like the bird! It lives on clean air and fresh water!'

How many lives would it take for us to no longer doubt?

YET ... THE DEUCE!

Despite this, however, there is something that I find very odd and contradictory in all this.

Let me explain.

Do people generally tend to wonder if the trees are really going green again in the spring? Of course, no! It's part of the regular things, the normal things in life.

If people easily accept this normal outcome, year after year, that means they have become accustomed – *without perhaps realizing it* – to make some kind of 'leap of faith'! They believe that the leaves will come back; they don't have the slightest doubt.

In short, they know how to *trust!* They are therefore able to believe! But why then did they not do it all the time?

They should equally believe that the Creator... or Buddha, or even that *the Forces of Life*, as said by Martin Gray, we reserve the best in all that we have to live every day. The beautiful, the great, the wonderful, should also be part of the so-called *normal* things of life! And that we should not worry about what life will bring us! As similarly, we don't care whether our trees will blossom again!

What is this aberration in wanting to choose the moments, the circumstances in which we should believe or not to believe?

In short, it's like saying 'I'm going to believe that spring will come back and it will serve me again all of its complex transformations, beautiful, wonderful, enigmatic; but I will not believe that life will continue to bring me what I need to be happy!' What a strange reasoning!

That's why I shouted above: When are we going to believe something beautiful, great, wonderful will happen to us? In sum, when are we going to believe the beautiful, the big, the wonderful, is *part* of the things in *normal* life... like the leaves coming back in the spring? And that the beautiful, the big, are definitely wonderful and available all the time.

But, again, as it feels forced, as it's uncomfortable to be so far from certain; and above all, as it's easy to find excuses or reasons by the bunch, it's hard to be convinced otherwise.

The fact of questioning me about the benefits of the experience that followed our couple of *poisoners*, is a fine example of the doubt that awaits us all.

Having noticed afterwards a lot of good things that our pests had pinned in their adventure, I should have believed right away.

Since then, I keep *an open mind*; I keep the *door of faith open!*

Second important point:

Give your 100%

There too, people are no more likely to want to make a constant effort today.

I make use here, of a reflection by Abraham Maslow, a great researcher in psychology, which advances that about *five percent* of people go to 'fully' in their work and in life in general. It assumes that the others, live by habit!

Can we expect then that life brings *all* to these beings, so unaccustomed to self-giving? We are far from the people who wisely use their thinking machine to attract the good things in life!

Have you ever heard of this thought: No *danger life gives me this ... or that!* Yet life is impersonal; life doesn't give by itself! But you, on the other hand, if you give your 100% (*your 110%, taking from great sportscasters*) it would seem that this same life, then, according to your way of thinking, should give you what you need to be happy.

I like to paraphrase John F. Kennedy, who said, 'Don't ask what your country can bring you... but instead ask yourself what you are willing to bring to your country!'

By transposing, one could say: *don't ask what life can bring us, but we ask rather what we are prepared to make in this life!* In life, it's *'give and take'* in some way. You give a lot, you take away a lot; you give little or nothing, you take away accordingly, that is to say, little or nothing...

Moreover, it's not, cursing this life or our past, *or even the government for that matter*, that we will attract the right things.

Note that I had a university colleague who had scored a zero, in an essay on the philosophy of work and effort, arguing, essentially, that neither effort nor the work was made for humans! 'The evidence, he said, these things *exhaust him*!'

We are well aware that the work is intended able to ennoble man, to make him able to make sense of his life. Yet there are many people who think that the formula of cheaters, profiteers, 'grumps' is much more profitable!

This philosophy of people who go to the easiest way out, while exploiting others, might just come from the fact that life spoils us and encourages us not to make any effort. See how today everything seems to work in an automatic way by buttons, by levers. Everywhere in the house, in the car, we want to do as in the well-known television program, *"Everybody speaks about it"* when the speaker says: Manon presses the button!

A few years ago, I found myself with plastic teeth and I wanted to buy some cream to polish and clean them. I was told, 'Don't bother! Put them to soak in a bowl with a *cleaning tablet*, and there you'll have it!'

You, who have natural teeth, don't laugh too much; with the speed of progress, who knows if one day you'll have to put your head in a bowl with a tablet, too!

Good! Let's go back to my sheep. Buttons, muttons ... get it?!

We said earlier, that we should live in expectation of receiving from life; believing that life brings us beautiful things, and that, it's *normal*.

At the same time, one must also understand that we have to practice positive thinking, mental cinema, etc. – *I'll elaborate later.*

.

Alas! This isn't what happens in general today. People would rather make small talk, procrastinate, analyze, criticize, and finally start *doubting*. Even if they are willing to understand that all these things that we talked about earlier could be in the realm of possibility, it's ultimately the ease of the *doubt* that outweighs the effort to *believe*. We don't want to put in the energy, we don't like to fight with ourselves. We would rather have magic recipes, any kind of placebo.

People are willing to take courses, read books, and attend workshops. But when they come out of a meeting or any talk, they will say that they fell down from their chair, they are speechless!

'Ah! It's really true what he says!'

But, from there to bother to make the effort to put this into practice, there is a huge margin!

When you read a good book, when you listen to a good chat, you can be stimulated, excited. If the speaker then says to you: 'Now go put it all into practice in your daily life; *go make the effort!*'

Obviously the temptation to neglect to take action would often be too present. This is where our strength of will is required; as well as our desire to move forward and lead ourselves.

Little 'asides'

It was at that moment that I understood a bit at least, 'one' of the great benefits of these group experiences, like the famous courses followed by my kind of zany; who also wanted me to get into his *enlightened* adventure, let us remember!

It looked to be a place where we stopped to suggest you to go and make the effort this week in your work, etc. It was a place where we rather say to you:

'You're making the effort right now! Tonight! Right here! Bang!'

A place where you're *caught off guard*, where you don't have time to analyze too long nor weigh the effectiveness of the methodology used too much, nor the time to consider *all so-called soft skills, as proposed by the Ministry of Education!*

In short! A real training place, practice, work; where you could do serious catching up after a long time, in all everyday situations, we set aside *effort*.

We live in a society that no longer values excellence; on the contrary, the high ground is left to those who are dragging their feet, to critics who whine or curse at life.

Moreover, it's surely because of this ongoing softness that so many people, not being very proud of themselves, eventually develop some unhappiness with all *internal parasites* that entails: bitterness, gloom, insomnia, to name a few. I have always believed that one who gives his all, did not have to get up at night to tinker, to knit, or take *pills*. This is the void that creates the daily insomnia.

In short, it did not seem at all to me as a niggling method; there is no hesitation. It is live! *Wham! In the buffet!*

Imagine if, in addition, this place became a place where no one had the choice to say no! A kind of formula in which you trust the method, accomplishing all that was asked of you, *or else you evacuate*, as said another.

Was not that a forceful way to get people to practice this famous trust?

If you accept to live through a lot of bizarre situations, if you agree to let yourself embark on a number of more or less ridiculous exercises, and for several evenings in front of lots of people, and at the end, you manage to not be stopped or even bothered by that same ridicule – *as I saw during that final gala* – would you not understand then how, in a similar way, it could almost be too easy, if not more, to accept the discomfort, uncertainty and aberrations that occur in what we live every day?

Think about it; what stops most people, is this fear of ridicule or looking ridiculous... 'How am I going to look?' 'What are they gonna say about me?' That's why people don't normally dare.

As long as we haven't put the *'fear of fear'* away, we will not get involved in life; and we cannot move forward.

The practice seems to be exercised in these group experiments, and it's precisely made for people who haven't had the chance to act out or have been bullied. They realize how it's easy to operate, when we're no longer worried about our image, when we *don't give a rat's ass* about the ridiculous. Trust is built, of course.

Note that to understand all this, it isn't too complicated; what is complicated, is to have the audacity and courage to seek to embark on such adventures, and being willing to make the effort. Such boldness isn't for everyone, for the reasons I explained above. Besides, where is the heroism these days?

Some rightly criticize the group experiments without much knowledge. They like to talk through their hats – *or rather nowadays, through their caps*, claiming that people don't need to compare, share, or learn from each other. They will prefer to have their own *shrink, their own coach, their own adviser!* In avoiding unfolding in front of others, they feel that they may be safe. But is it certain that the benefit due to the individual work of a psychologist or a *coach*, will not show up as quickly as the one resulting from the involvement of a large number of people working together? The addition of all the results of each group member would it not foreseeable impact the advice of a single individual?

All that remains to be seen, of course; but I'm not ready to condemn such actions. Facilitators who work with groups have the same concerns as clinical specialists. In both cases, officials want to get people to believe in themselves, to believe in life.

I just talked of *one* of the great benefits this *particular* adventure produces. There are others, naturally. I'm thinking especially of all the exceptional situations which are lived in the group. These, we cannot describe unless we experience them.

The curious and thirsty for the great human exchanges, *be warned!*

3RD IMPORTANT POINT:

Quiet confidence…

In short, in these kinds of courses or otherwise, you have to get to the end, to install *the quiet confidence* in you. It will then be easy to focus on the essential, that is to say, the beautiful, the great and wonderful that must fill our lives!

The secret will be to be able to successfully develop a large and steady *naïveté* about all that we encounter on our way. A kind of quiet confidence *that must surely be a good reason behind each of the more or less questionable situations we constantly face.*

This is like going its way innocently with the certainty that his '*car is on the driveway.*'

Your car's on the driveway!

Ah, see? You haven't heard of that one! 'Your car's on the driveway!' comes from our unique and deep Bernard. Bernard was a fellow employee at the time.

One evening, Denis, was prowling around Bernard, repeating that he would be chosen to be part of a training group. Since he resumed his attack often, he had Bernard then used this memorable phrase on him.

Bernard spoke in parables. *Another one!* It was only much later, Denis, understood the meaning of this very profound reflection: 'Your car's on the driveway!'

When your faith is absent, as with Denis that night, you try to convince yourself, you speak abundantly: 'I will be chosen! I will be chosen!' But when you're full of confidence, and that you expect that thing to happen to you, you don't talk. You know, somehow, that it will happen to you.

Bernard wanted to point out to Denis that he was not at all worried about returning home at the end of the evening, as outside his car was there, *waiting at the door*. He didn't need to speak about it; it was a sure thing.

However, on the other hand, why did he repeat that mantra so often, about how he would be chosen if he was so convinced of it happening?

In sum, our beliefs bleed from our character and, sooner or later, will show in our behavior.

Indeed, Denis was not convinced enough, confident enough. He did not have *the quiet confidence*. He had no faith!

Besides, he was not chosen to be part of the group! His car was not '*in the driveway*'!

4TH MAJOR AND IMPORTANT POINT:

Confidence!

I want to tell you an old not so funny story; it's even a little sad.

As René Lévesque said, one day: *'Wait until I remember!'*

It's the story of Arthur, the good farmer who sowed his fields, and was rocking on his balcony while watching his wheat grow! – *Each to his own!* – The priest or the doctor, or even the *beggar* came by. At the time, in the countryside, everyone ended up passing by; especially the *attracted beggar*! It's not for nothing that many people still have in their porch, a replica of the famous *collector's chest* – for *'le quéteux'* it was said before. A bench that could be opened, and in which one put a little anything during the year: knitted items, warm clothes, shoes, all kinds of useful things, so this itinerant beggar, father of all the homeless of this world, can spend the winter warm.

'You will have a real good crop,' he was told.

Arthur was rocking, and religiously smoked his old blackened pipe, while nodding.

'Yeah! The wind, hail, will eventually strike me down!'

I have often told this story in my conference rooms. I think this is where people would have laughed. But I have never heard the people guffaw over it. That's why I say it's probably not a very funny story.

Let's carry on

.

When autumn came, and the wheat came along, chubby, brown, ready to burst – *in fact, Arthur had an awful harvest; he had to store his grain at the neighbors, so much it overflowed. He had to change tractors two or three times, to cushion its profits! (As you see, I happen to exaggerate on occasion, but not so much nowadays!)* – When the autumn came, I say, people came by and said again:

'That was some great harvest!'

And Arthur replied:

'That kind of harvest, makes no damn good sense! That will dry my land for good, and I'll never reap something good!'

And, much like now, just a few giggles forced into the room. That's why I added further up, that it was quite the sad story!

Laughter is the product of contrast: the *big chubby face* against *little shrimp*, Laurel's whimsy against Hardy's realism, the ease of a race against an unexpected obstacle, the evidence of success in the face of *the refusal to see it*, the sure-fire *normal crop* insured against the *improbable catastrophe*! The eloquent contrast should have been funny! But when one doesn't have faith, we will not see the striking contrasts; you cannot see anything funny in there.

When are we going to believe that something beautiful, great, wonderful…

I repeat it again; of course, this is my *motto*!

Following this banal anecdote, however, a kind of *flash* came to my mind.

To be embarrassed, shy, all wrong, like a cucumber, as I have already said, isn't necessarily the only reason that prevents people from being happy. I think the essence of happiness would rather come when you're confident in life?

How come the funny farmer, probably an experienced one, very experienced, I should say, is no longer *certain* to have other good harvests? He, who still believes that the trees don't have the choice of coming to life, in spring? He should know that the success of his future harvest is part of the *normal* things of life?

Basically, when you're embarrassed, shy, frustrated, anxious, of course, swimming your way to happiness won't be easy! But these are things that can be corrected.

To be embarrassed to the point of waiting for his wife in the car, a whole evening, while the heater doesn't work, by the bitter cold, just because we are afraid to come face to people, I agree, is a *nasty unnecessary suffering*!

To be arrogant to the point of breaking everything in the house to prove to his wife that you are right is also an unnecessary suffering! To be anxious, nervous, (anxious,) sleepless... are also sufferings. They never have (never) made anyone happy, and have brought nothing to humanity either. Anyway, it's always unnecessary sufferings. No one is required to live a life, overwhelmed by such obstacles. Of course in some cases, some therapy will help you to rid yourself of all these afflictions.

But, even if embarrassed by these kinds of difficulties, it would be nothing compared to the fact of not having faith. *'There'*, it would be bad! *'There'*, you'd be really stuck!

But people don't realize their lack of positive attitude; their eyes are too glued to their woes, their diseases, their unnecessary sufferings. Some even tend to glorify them. See how it became almost snobbery than having had problems, to have been sick or having surgery.

'I had surgery *four times!*' I've also gone through two nervous breakdowns!'

Then, taking a serious tone, they add:

'And I'm now going to my third!'

At the same time, it gives them the necessary justification and easy excuse to accept that nothing will change. See all the *'Oh! Only if'!* Ah! Only if I were rich! Ah! Only if I was educated, beautiful, big, strong!

All this illustrates that someone who doesn't want too much bother, will always find excuses! But we know that *'one'* who wants things strongly, finds ways!

And, it doesn't mean you have all the cards to play to succeed. Wealth, education, beauty, is not absolute guarantees to success. You may have read as I have that *what is important isn't so much to have a good hand, but play well the one that we have!*

Many educated people, many beautiful stars, rich, famous, have even committed suicide. Yet they seemed to have everything going for them: fame, material abundance...

Probably we were too influenced by the culture of our neighbor, the American giant.

The Biggest of the World

'*To be happy, you need such a house in such a place... this big car, such finery.*'

In the end, those are all just masks.

With or without masks, I still believe that we must continually be in possession of the *quiet confidence* which I mentioned before – the assurance that we are made to be happy.

Can we imagine an inconsequential Creator who only give this privilege to a few? We can all enjoy life *to the fullest*! Except that to get there, we must believe. We have to have *faith*, we must *trust!*

Not the kind of trust that makes you looking good, like a hotshot; but like that of the little child sleeping soundly, knowing that tomorrow he will eat. He knows that his parents will take care of him; he'll have for his birthday a *yellow and black* bicycle. And he will! While his parents are not yet fully convinced!

I will always remember the Boutin guy I met on a Sunday morning at the door of a bakery with forty loaves in his cart.

'Good God in heaven! Can you eat bread!'

'Not really! I am alone with my wife! It's to put in the freezer! They said on the radio that there would be a strike at the millers!'

It's been 60 years since the man eats every day, and that morning, he loses faith in a snap!

Life is a bit *like a cruise*. In a cruise, you don't even think to ask the captain if he believes he will lead us safely. We don't think; we are convinced. Why then, in the cruise of our lives, are we still so worried? Why so much fear of the future in today's world? We make strikes for a possible security. We buy all kinds of insurance. It's a game of cards. We are looking at the stars... In short we forget to keep the little child sleeping soundly.

We must find ways to regain that *trust* we unfortunately lost in the face of the daily negatives. As did the father Boutin, sometimes.

Now, let's talk about these daily negatives. See how we have full-page spreads of misfortunes on newspapers; how television operates on gloom, disaster. Even soap operas are impregnated with, 'What kind of misfortune will be served to us tonight?' The negative is fashionable. Tell someone that you are well, you will hardly be interesting. Tell your problems, your misfortunes, at a party, you will become popular.

How many movements do you think have been done in Quebec with the aim of helping people; hundreds, thousands? Almost as many as there are difficulties: *big* eaters, *heavy* drinkers, singles, mental conditions, abused, divorced, single parents, slightly battered, heavily battered ... in short, I cannot name them all anyway!

So don't be surprised if our comedians are a booming business! With all this gloom, this invasive sadness, people have come *to pay* for laughter, as living has become such a heavy burden! See how some 'three for one' humor packages sell well!

With the negative education we received at home, at school, at church and for the elderly, we don't have to be surprised so much havoc in our minds.

'Don't touch that! Don't do that!'

Only the clichés have followed us: Born with nothing! We are not rich, but we are honest!

We are likely to remain honest, if we say it so much! We risk not being rich at all either!

Try it for yourself! Ask someone how he is... He will certainly answer: 'Not bad... Not so bad... Not too bad... Not worse off... It could be better!'

No danger in him being well! The people have gone there!

Yeah! But...

What would it take just to counter this negative attitude, this attitude of worry and misery? What should we do to be able to develop enthusiasm and confidence to live?

The answer is that we should come to install the certainty that success, achievement, that it should be drilled into *your noggin*, to quote my grandmother!

Success, the joy of living, security, are not guaranteed by the accumulation of many material goods, nor a lot of labor contracts, nor permanence or even by armored wall to wall insurance policies.

We need success, happiness, security in life, a kind of *state of spirit*, a kind of *state of mind!* Which state of mind should be innate in us; one in which state of mind should testify, assert that one is *made* absolutely for success, for achievement, for happiness; that it's part of (and I say it again) the *normal* things in life!

We must find once and for all, this positive attitude that our daily lives suffocate too often, the art of being good with oneself and with others as said by Mr. Theo Chantrier, over the radio once. An art of living well with yourself first, *and then* with the other, he liked to repeat.

Surely as always, there can be no *thirty-six* ways to achieve happiness. But what matters above all is to take action to regain the confidence that lived when you were very young, *when you slept soundly, knowing that tomorrow, etc.* The idea is no longer to listen to yourself; especially those who tend to shut their large ears, well down, before you could hear yourself complain.

So that's why I would like to stress both on the internal state that we must develop.

5th Important point:

We are unique!

Confidence comes when I discover that I am unique. None among the billions of people on earth have my character traits, nor my fingerprints or my DNA; so I am singular, I'm special!

Those who tend to diminish upon facing someone who's stronger, more beautiful or more fortunate, just think of the giant I mentioned before, and tell you that even in this *big country,* if someone visits *Ausable Chasm,* for example,   walking in the gorges of the place where it's dark, where there is very little dry ground, otherwise the rock, you should see almost leafless trees, and drying buds.

We are far quite far from the famous '*Biggest of the World!*' This isn't even comparable to pretty leafy birch at *Uncle Diogène's camping,* in Saint-Félix-de-Kingsley.

At the same time, however, one might think that these trees *seem* very far from success, while the beautiful birches of Saint-Félix are close. Let's not fool ourselves here. These tiny shrub species that have never seen the full light or the fattened ground succeed anyway to grow through the stone of the barely lit caverns. Isn't this an extraordinary success?

There! So is the same for humans! When will we be aware of our values, and what we can bring to life and to those around us, despite our smallness and our limitations? With our meager branches on stony ground, or our large foliage shading the green! (*Gee! it's almost like Victor Hugo!*)

Behind it all, however, what matters is that we are inhabited by some *purpose* on this earth!

It would be terrible if we wake up and we got up to go by *wandering*, as I said, further, muttering that kind of thinking:

'Well, well, look at that! I woke up this morning!'

Alas! People get up by *dragging* themselves, then go round and round all day complaining that nothing is happening in their lives, then, go to bed at night, dissatisfied with themselves. So don't be surprised, they are hardly able to sleep well. How can they *snooze* soundly, not expecting much from life?

6TH IMPORTANT POINT:

WHAT'S YOUR GOAL?

What did they do during this important day, apart from being worried and have ruminated their weak, almost useless state?

On the contrary, those who are motivated by a great goal, and seek success, will be very busy, and thus sleep well. And they know that to achieve their great purpose, while relatively far, and so as not to be discouraged, they will have to go sometimes by a series of smaller goals that eventually lead them to realize their great first goal.

Therefore, before you travel – *which could be my own goal further at the end of the line* – I have to prepare my passport, my luggage, book my plane, my hotel room, tell my wife – so she doesn't look for me during my absence! Small easy-to-reach goals!

Why should it be any different in life? Before you think to be happy one day, why not do little things immediately to become happy?

And those I mentioned earlier, those circling, being concerned about their misfortunes, will they come to understand that they should change their *concerns* and *preoccupations into occupations?* A person who is engaged, busy, has no time to look for *internal problems – for bugs*, as we say!

It's also said that the child *aspires to become an adult...* 'Me can!' he says. He knows perhaps not combine his verbs, and pronouns, but has in him the desire to already *be big*! Sometimes I wonder if in general the adult continues to aspire to become big?

Have you ever seen a child learning to walk? He falls to the ground, tumbling into the bottom of the basement, back to tumble again, cries, but gets up and starts again! I've never met a child who exclaimed:

'*The devil take me, I won't walk anymore!*'

But no; he gets up and starts again! So what? The strength that was in us when we were children, that forced us to get up and start over, shouldn't have disappeared?

Why do adults discourage so easily? Why are we constantly apologizing, and barely make the effort it takes to avoid being given the pink slip?

Wasn't it Lincoln who said that *people are happy as far as they decided to be*!

I knew very little about Lincoln... I knew he was a great man, I knew he was President of the United States, he had managed to abolish slavery; in short, *that's* almost everything I knew about him. But by digging, I discovered that this man *had* been *fed up*, as they say, many times in his life.

Did you know that at 31 years old, he began his public life by going bankrupt? When he was 32, after presenting himself as candidate for the parliamentary elections, he lost? Two years later he went bankrupt again? When he was 35, he saw his girlfriend die, which plunged into a severe depression?

Bankrupt in business, bankrupt in politics, bankrupt as well in his personal life!

'Nothing works,' he could've said. '*I don't want to play anymore!*'

But no! It begins again – and again, he bites the dust at 36, 43, 48!

Of course he continued to be known and to advance in his public life; but he met appalling failures!

He missed his shot in the Senate seven years later. He couldn't succeed in being accepted as vice president of the United States the following year, only to be beaten again in the Senate, at 58 years old.

Finally, it was not until the age of 60, after thirty years of effort, dotted with at least a dozen stinging refusals, he managed to get elected as president of the United States of America!

That's what he meant when he said that people are happy *as far as they decide to be!*

But as I said in some way further, people seek happiness in the stars, in four-leaf clovers... they wait for a miracle. They don't know that *when there isn't a thing left to do, there is still something to do!*

Like Lincoln, we can all at some point, experience a kind of discouragement. Our case is *so sad*! We feel lonely, *abandoned by life! We're so pitiful!* Then comes our big ears – *as I said earlier* – that we unfold carefully, the better to hear our own moaning, with all the indulgence and meekness we deserve!

Until the day we understand that instead of bawling on our poor fates, we must instead put the focus on the positive part of our balance sheets. I know it's not always easy to see the bright side of things. The temptation to give in to despondency is often very strong.

How many people, if they had been in Lincoln's place, would rather be discouraged and given up? How many people daily are dragging their feet, seeking an excuse to not go?

'I have a headache, I have a plow to try out, to tame a bull ...' Finally, I mix things up a bit, but you know the parable!

All that to say, that when *you must, you must*! If you're wanted somewhere, and if you got beheaded, then, *put your head under your arm and move your feet*! For someone who *really wants it*, there isn't a thing that can stop them.

Of course, I still rehash the same ideas. *'What do you want?' Jean Chrétien would say!* It's always my good old professorial habits that come back to me, and remind me constantly, that the message sticks well when you repeat it!

7TH IMPORTANT POINT:

The world all around you?

Yeah! That's a point to consider: *your environment!*

Indeed the environment in which we live in influences us greatly.

It's like if the example of others, added to their daily attitude, and their common thoughts, eventually rub off in some way, then join us and mark us.

Guglielmo Marconi, the inventor of the wireless radio – *some would say that it's rather Fessenden. In fact, it was Marconi who sent the first, a one-way message beyond the Atlantic. Fessenden was the first to make the round trip.* Regardless, Marconi, I say, explains that our thoughts are traveling much like waves. It's as if we have within us a kind of transmitter and a kind of receiver. We send out and we attract waves.

Besides who has not experimented with telepathy? For example, the phone will ring simultaneously when we're about to call someone; and that is exactly when *someone* is on the line! '*Hey! I was just about to call you!*' Or, that two or more people are surprised to mean the same thing at the same time! *They are on air*!

This is even more evident in the small child whose thinking isn't yet completely autonomous. When he took his first steps, get a number of you watching and whisper among yourselves: 'He will fall! He will fall!' and he might just take a dive!

Like me, you have seen families, accustomed to unemployment and abject poverty for generations!

Probably because these people have always lived with the *conviction* that they will never come out of it. Much like the wife who is convinced that her man will always go to the tavern!

The *poor* man (!) who has no will and is attracted by the *divine* bottle, feels like *pushed* towards the bar by the thoughts of his wife! The lady isn't responsible of course; but it doesn't help! She must have mental images of her man coming home to *gently get drunk! To take a beer or two, I mean*!

Why has there always been so much unemployment, and a lot of sick people with us? Because we have too long been *assured* of having them! With the former '*Unemployment insurance*' and '*Illness insurance*', we thought unemployment and sickness. '*Employment insurance*' and '*health insurance*' are two new concepts that are just starting to settle into our thinking.

Our beliefs bleed from us; it's a form of magnetism. It will therefore monitor our thoughts. Many sages and philosophers have argued consistently that *we bring into our lives what we have in our thoughts!*

One of my teachers even said: we don't always have what we *deserve* in life; on the other hand, more often than not, *we reap what we think about*! This is a reflection that hits hard!

Johann Wolfgang von Goethe, German playwright, went further. He said we *have to treat people as if they were what they 'should' be*, and so we would help them to become what they are *truly capable of being*!

To understand, consider the following example.

Someone who has the habit of treating his children as little monsters, as unruly, and who, continually would talk to his peers:

'I'll tell you what my second kid just did, that little rascal! Etc'

That someone, I say, would end up by acting in this way, by pushing a little more each time, on the way to indiscipline, and to *dissipation*! Whereas if that same person saw them, with a calmer thought, successfully, it could help them to become a calm person! Good vibes go around somehow!

All this isn't magic; it's not instantaneous. But we have seen many situations where parents came to surprising results.

On the other hand, it takes much more than *wishes* to draw conclusive results. It takes conviction! Too many people don't know what they want or don't really want. They therefore don't emit much since their small personal transmitter doesn't attract more.

The older will remember Jean Drapeau. This man did not *expect* to have a subway one day. *'Tomorrow,'* he said, *'we dig!'*

It's certain that we meet extinguishers on our way. There are even species of specialists able to easily find *the big pet peeve,* when it's not just some *fly, some speck,* bothering us to the point of discouragement.

What about some journalists, from the newspapers, the radio or even on television, who are trained to make mountains out of molehills, thanks to their well rehearsed machine. They will never *know that progress is being made by those who do things and not by those who discuss how they should have been doing!*

I remember Kathy Kreiner, a young Ontario skier who won the gold medal at the Olympic Games in Innsbruck in 1976. But there was a headline in the newspaper saying: *The journalists didn't even bother!* They had probably said:

'Who's that Kathy Kreiner? I don't know, I'll just stay in bed!'

Then she won the gold medal during their absence!

It's therefore very fortunate that they didn't bother! Negative as they used to be, she might not have won anything. Their vibes going, *'She won't make it! She'll fall!'* would probably have ended up influencing her.

It was the same with Sylvie Bernier, in Los Angeles in 1984.

One of those journalists, doubt-mongers, came in for commentary, tried to allude to another diver who teetered dangerously close to her *score*. Sylvie then put her Walkman headphones on her ears and yelled almost brutally him:

'I don't care! I'll go get the gold medal!'

And get it, she did!

Who are these critics, these freeloaders, these doomsayers? What do they do that's so important? Aside from ranting, convicting and undoing our stars: Céline Dion, Jacques Villeneuve, even our deceased Expos.

A big mouth *polluted* the airwaves with his art criticisms. After the young Céline sang the national anthem for the first time at the Olympic Stadium, he said:

'She's nothing impressive… apart from a small waterfall in her voice!'

The same big fatty had also said of Andrea Bocelli:

'He won't go far with his *little* voice!'

Fortunately, the Kathy Kreiners and the Sylvie Berniers of the world knew how to practice strong *visualisation*. Thus, by being in the process to win their victories, they greatly helped themselves, not only to reach their goals, but at the same time they managed to destroy and neutralize *negative* vibes.

This kind of visualization, this mental cinema, is basically an application of the *mental attitude* which I mentioned at the beginning of this book. Taking the attitude of a winner is acting like a winner, doing actions like a winner. It's also thinking like a winner. And through repetition, you start acting and creating this new desired habit.

Notice that we, *ordinary mortals*, have in our daily lives, our specialised extinguishers, which are lively and ready to criticize our conduct. We should also adjust our headphones and carry on; so as not to hear these *pseudo-helpers* who want to flood us with their fears, their ghosts, and their *pseudo-knowledge*!

My father said in his speech of old:

'Don't listen to the 'know-alls' who try to flood you with their 'knowledge-alls'!'

It meant everything.

All this only delays our success.

'If you had to stop at all the barking dogs,' my grandmother used to say... – *I don't remember too much of the rest of her maxim... Anyway!*

Considering that we are constantly invaded by radio, TV and newspapers, when we become the showcase of so much misery and so many disasters, it becomes easier for our imagination, the *Queen of the house*, to set into motion, and create every journalistic assault while a scenario, while a negative mental film, may then be transposed into our own lives.

To better understand, let us pause for a moment over the famous topic of health. It will be very easy to see that, here too, we face a huge influence in the game of advertising. We are constantly bombarded by multiple announcements of diseases and drugs.

Nowadays, we have dictionaries of *symptoms*! Imagine! When you experience any discomfort, you look in the book, and you'll discover a range of diseases that may contain your discomfort among the original symptoms.

Isn't that amazing! Isn't it *'beautiful'*! Would say *'Les têtes à claques'*!

Soon, people will eventually listen all day in search of a *beautiful* disease. And when they have found it, they will all be impressed, and while shivering, they begin to analyze it. From there, it will be quite easy and natural to come to discuss the concern, and ultimately to be of *bad blood*, in the words of Dr. Albert. The act of worrying, to think about it, to feel things, is also the surest way to attract more anything that resembles the famous disease!

In this same line of thought, trying to understand how it could be disturbing for a person with a fertile imagination, to be told fortunes, even when things aren't so bad.

'*You'll probably get stomach problems,*' says the seer.

And the person, from that moment will not know quite how to eat or what to eat.

He just continues to mull over his concerns – *so to say* – and I would not be surprised that he would eventually attract all sorts of digestive problems. *And as to dramatize, why not be soon on the edge of a surgery?*

8TH IMPORTANT POINT:

THE POWER OF THOUGHT

Dr. Murphy said that *regardless of the object of our faith*, it eventually works! Deeply believe that coffee prevents us from sleeping, and we give an order to our subconscious mind to stay awake.

The thoughts we have inside will also give orders to our subconscious, somewhat in the same way.

When the internal message is addressed to ourselves, to our own person, it's called this form of thought, of 'autosuggestion'. You know the principle; continuously repeat an idea and it eventually get printed in us.

If at least one always has a mantra of positive ideas, such a, 'I am able, I am confident, I can still manage everything, etc...'! Alas, too often it's the Groundhog drivel, to the tune of: 'Hey! I'm so stupid!' Or: 'I'm telling you, it's not gonna work!'

Note that, at least, until there, we're talking about treating yourself. Even if the effect is harmful, it happens at home, inside you only. But too often, our messages, like I said earlier, are way beyond us and try somehow to influence others. It then becomes a form of direct suggestion. If everything was expressed by the means of encouraging words that would be great; as for example: '*C'mon, you can do it!*' But when it's rather disparaging remarks, critics, reproaches, the effect will be unfortunately very different.

And the whole can be more subtle yet. I refer to this form any *transmission of thought, telepathy*, that some use almost continuously.

We may not always be trying to say to our children that they are brilliant, extraordinary, or even that they are morons or idiots! But suppose that this idea gets us in the head pretty much all the time – *you see me coming with my big felt boots, coffee brown, etc.* Yes sir! We would help them to become *great* or on the contrary, to become *ugly*. According to the way we see them, and always according to the explanation of Von Goethe. Remember, we talked about him above.

It reminds me of the story of Cléophas and Phonsine, a simple example, to illustrate the influence of the thought.

Let's start with Cléophas.

He was a *slacker*, a *bum*, who vegetated in his corner. He found no employment. On the other hand, whenever he thought of moving, and he approached the door jamb to go check out a 'maybe' the possibility to work. His wife, Exidrille, cried out:

'You still want to go *wasting your time*? You degenerate; just stay there, then. You know that you'll never find anything! *'Loser!'*

And this was for years.

Finally, one day, Cléophas disappeared from *civilization*! It was not a too big loss for the village, I tell you that. I'll come back to that in a bit.

There was a similar story somewhere else with a certain Phonsine, *the 'slacker'* from another village…

From time to time, we could see her hurtle down the side to get to the corner shops – *I should say, tumbled down to the lowest shops, so she was without any widespread form!* – A woman with several floors: a floor of curls, a floor of jacket, a floor of old socks. She also disappeared one day from her hometown.

Let's say, for brevity, that several years later, people eventually saw Cléophas again.

'But if it isn't Cléophas!' said some.

'But, no! It cannot be!' added others.

Well dressed, very elegant, it was actually our Cléophas!

'But that happened? We could no longer recognize you!'

And Cleophas answered:

'I changed wives! My poor Exidrille (*God rest her soul!*) continually saw me as a *loser*, as insignificant; I therefore tended to be. Now with my new wife, I tell myself that I am great, I am able. I have almost no other choice to be!

And it was the same for Phonsine.

When they saw her again, ten years later, hair done very well, very elegant in her heavily tailored suit – *I'll grace you with my gestures* – all also asked heaps of questions. She also explained how her previous man saw her as *backward*, and good for nothing.

'"Get out so there! Fatso! You can't do anything!" he told me every day.

'He wouldn't even let me go answer the door by myself; he had such little trust in me! (*God rest his soul!*)'

My new husband, never tired of complimenting me, and always sees me as extraordinary. And I became so more and more, almost despite myself.

Good! In conclusion, it does not mean to bring our husbands and our women to death to become someone! It's an anecdote that isn't so bad in *telling*, but we should realize that the way one sees the other should help them, as said Von Goethe, *to become who or what they are capable of being.*

Alas! Today we no longer want to go to this trouble. At the slightest annoyance, we break everything, we divorce or separate, it's easier!

When I was sometimes reporting the comments of people who said: '*But if it isn't Cléophas*,' or '*But if it isn't Phonsine*', I was reminded of an old joke of the poet-singer Georges Langford, when he taught somewhere in New Brunswick.

A student told him in the middle of class:

'*M'sieu*! I just came across a "joual" in the school yard!' What means of course, a 'horse' in French slang.

And Georges responded:

'But no! It was a *cheval,* my little Paul. We say 'CHEVAL!'

The student had been to reflect a few moments, then had resumed sententious:

But Sir! It really looked like a *joual!*

Good! Let's go back *to our horses, to our sheep*, as I'd like to say. It's good to see others as one would like them to be, to help them become what they are capable of being. However, similarly, we should understand that we have just as much the possibility *to see us capable of being one or that we want to be*! We have to do our mental cinema; seeing us becoming what we have chosen to be.

Cases of mental movies or visualizing, if you prefer, used in loads of people who have experienced success, are too common and too many for one to reject the effectiveness. Examples we have seen in sportsmen, politicians, or renowned artists.

We have specifically stressed the utilization of this visualization with Sylvie Bernier in the previous chapter as well as the results it gave.

However, it's unfortunate as she confessed it in an interview on her return from Beijing; she had to hide her books of *positive thinking* during her participation at the Los Angeles Games. She did not want people to mock her, being the only one of the group to believe in the power of thought; she was also *the only one* of the group to win the gold medal! *It's good enough to talk about!*

9TH IMPORTANT POINT:

The main course: Psychosomatic life!

We all want, surely, for things to be swell, not only in our lives in general – *that is to say, in our work, in our married life, in our family life* – but we also want things to be well within our own person, in our *minds* and in our *frame*. Being good in your frame is to feel good about you as they say, is obviously a major asset. That should encourage a certain joy of living Liberation and enthusiasm, to better achieve.

But this inner well-being isn't easy to install. There are indeed all around us, negative vibes of which I spoke. These negative vibes, in the long run, could wreak havoc and gradually affect, at first, our mental attitude, our state of mind. Let us remember the gloom lurking everywhere and watching us!

One can easily understand that if our mind is so shaken and weakened, it could, afterwards, rub off and affect our frame, too.

Wasn't it Obelix who said, 'When appetite goes, everything goes!' We can also understand that if *things go well inside*, appetite will be waiting for you.

Where I want to get, is that we have to realize in the end, there is a strong relationship and interdependence of *conscious* life, and *unconscious* life. Between life of what is thought and life of what works alone. Between the life that comes from the soul, spirit – *the Psychological life* – and life that comes from physical, from the frame – *the Somatic life*.

That's why scientists use the term *psychosomatic* fairly regularly, just to illustrate the close relationship between these two aspects of ourselves: the *psychic* aspect and *somatic* – or *physical* – aspect that's the same thing.

How does it work?

There! We have the deepest part of our being, a principle of life, an *animus*, a sort of *master of our inner life* within us and that drives us. This *animus*, this inner strength, on one hand is always active initially in the machinations of our conscious mind. This force can activate our thinking machine, allowing us to reason, make judgments; so it accompanies our decision making.

On the other hand, that same inner strength is as much present when it comes to running the other life, unconscious life of our being – the part that *walks alone*.

Thus it takes care of my frame. It knows very well how to take care of my digestion, the circulation of my blood, the '*growth*' of my hair. This inner strength can even foster or hinder the healing of my wounds; depending on whether or not it's programmed correctly.

Furthermore, I would even imagine that *this force, this animus, this master of our lives* is a little part of the *Grand Master of life in general*.

I'm not the only one who has with me a force which acts as a force that powers my mind – a force that circulates my blood or regulates my heart beat.

You, like me, when we cut a finger, we find the *inner strength* to put in motion to heal everything. Surprisingly, it's as if this powerful magician was not only present in me, but in you, and in all, eventually. Since the same 'little miracle' occurs in all wounded beings! I can even say that this inner strength even knows how to stop so that the skin doesn't grow to the ground!

And to 'push' my thought further, I am convinced that this power, which is in me, and in you – *which is everywhere* – and might be called the *master of life*, is in all of us, a kind of ultimate power beyond the many small daily physiological acts that I just mentioned, that is to say: repair of the frame, digestion, blood circulation, etc. This large intelligent force, that wonderful strength, probably wants as the supreme goal, that we remain in perfect health of course, but at the same time that we become totally radiant, quite full of *'joie de vivre'* and quite overflowing in harmony.

Why then, stop believing in it, stop trust in it? Why put a spoke in the wheel in this *master of life*, thinking too often all sorts of negative things?

When we soak our mountains of problems, potential misfortunes, unnecessary sufferings, we end up messing up, curbing this master of life in us, preventing him from doing his job. We no longer think health, harmony or joie de vivre, as *he*, wishes. We are talking about diseases, hypothetical disasters, terrible fears, sometimes even up to chilling our entire being, giving it the same time and often a sneaky way around sink into the negative, that of lingering to failure, disease, and imbalance.

A SMALL DIGRESSION …

One day I met a traveler who explained that the existence of the *Master of life* in this way, with very little *thought*.

This *Master of life* in me, he said, is also in you, in plants; everywhere else. In each wonder of life, there is a force, a small engine. For example, the one in the tree, makes it grow, grows its leaves. This engine is driven by a larger one, which produces light, rain, activating the little engine making leaves and trees. This engine is itself operated by an even larger one, which in turn, rotates the stars. It's sort of a *generator engine of light and seasons*, but at the same time that these stars are holding up well suspended in the cosmos…

My character went on at length to explain his allegory, to arrive finally to say, there needs to be at all costs, a *giant engine* held somewhere to run it all! Him, he called, '*the full engine giant!*'

Such was his explanation, random guy style. He's real, the Grand Master who lives everywhere and in us; we sometimes call God, Buddha, Mohammed or the *Forces of life*, according to the favorite expression of Martin Gray.

THOUGHT VS FRAME

I was about to say now that we should *not put* '*roadblocks*' to this inner strength, maintaining negative ideas, that is.

This fact is, these ideas or these thoughts, if you like, that *eventually provoke reactions* in our *frame*. If we were inhabited by nice ideas, it would be extraordinary. The child happy at the *thought* of eating his favorite dessert, the beloved who rejoices and exalts himself going up to his sweetheart, the future Olympic medalist who sees success in the last steps of his race, all three because they are inhabited by joyful *thoughts* or *ideas*, promote an internal chemistry that is good for their frame.

If all people could cultivate, more often than not, these motivational ideas, they would be assured of being transported by a very good adrenaline generating mental and physical health.

But too often, unfortunately, people tend to feed on negative thoughts.

Try to imagine how it can become detrimental to a *sensitive* and *impressionable* person, to binge throughout the year, in woes, problems, or reading newspapers or listening to the radio or watching television!

Certainly in this situation, where we allow ourselves be assaulted by the negative, may end up generating an upheaval in our mood, and even in the balance of our physical health, as was pointed out above.

Having bad blood!

And if, in addition to feeding all the misfortunes of others through our wonderful television, these same people are also fed on their own inner poisons? I speak of poisons that some people often tend to drag for years, like *non-acceptance, constant frustration, resentment, hatred, or even thoughts of revenge.*

Couldn't this end up disturbing their beautiful interior balance? Their emotional *stasis*... We'll come back to this.

On the other hand, sometimes, I affirmed that inner strength handled somehow my digestion, the circulation of my blood and all the other activities listed inside of me.

I guess you don't believe that, at will, *consciously*, we could give an order to that inner strength, so it suddenly starts to accelerate our bloodstream, or hastens for example, the digestion of our last meal? *'Go, inner strength, step on it! I want my digestion done faster tonight!'*

Surely not!

However, try to imagine a different situation.

Suppose we were on a boat in distress, close to sinking, and that we don't know how to swim! *The thought* of dying by falling into the water could then make our hearts *beat wildly* and ensure that we become completely flooded by *sweat*?

Similarly, for a good piece of chocolate, a good steak or a glass of wine on the table could easily give us the thought or *idea – always same reasoning –* of a good treat, a good snack at hand soon? Which would put in motion the mechanisms and chemistry salivation: our olfactory nerves would start to quiver, our taste buds and our salivary glands get all excited!

On the other hand, if we place ourselves in a situation where we would neither be sinking, nor in the sight of chocolate, or steak on the table, we would not have these particular reactions in our frame; no profuse sweat, no heart racing, no salivation.

You will have realized that it's the thought, the concept, the idea of chocolate, wine or drowning, which will spontaneously cause the reactions described above.

Try to imagine now what kinds of reactions could result in us, if the ideas of *non-acceptance, hatred, resentment, revenge*, as I said above, if continuously, for years, kept in our gut. We certainly would not have more saliva in the mouth, or faster blood flow; but it's clear that over time, we might be invaded by a strange chemistry, quite sneaky and unhealthy, that many people have called in a manner entirely appropriate, by the expression – I repeat again – *'Getting bad blood'*

Moreover, many dermatologists often spoke of certain frame reactions that would be due mainly to the *non-acceptance* of a situation, for example, or other resentments maintained unabated.

It makes you wonder if cancer isn't sometimes a manifestation of 'extreme' inner reactions to *these toxic thoughts, these resentments* that we carry for years.

10TH IMPORTANT POINT:

A FUNNY WAY FOR THINKING?

I understand why Saint Francis, in a known prayer invites us to bring harmony where there is discord; pardon where there is error; to bring love where there is hatred...

In college, we were taught that same philosophy found in the famous prayer. Later, in contact with certain writings of Institute Jean XXIII, we found the same speech. Acceptance, forgiveness, love.

HOW DOES IT GO?

In our daily lives, we have to continually stir lots of images. These images are created from situations, *beautiful or less beautiful,* that we live through. We then archive them in our minds, in our memory. Using our thinking machine, we transform these images into concepts, into ideas... Our imagination distorts, makes them more or less attractive, 'Ah! As it would be *nice* if...' or more or less appalling, *'If it could happen* to me...'

Then comes the power of reasoning; we will be submitted then to all kinds of proposals, all kinds of scenarios. And, as we have an optimistic or pessimistic attitude, we'll desire, or fear of taking action. I simplify, of course.

That's why it's important to do the cleanup in our thoughts, and to encourage those that could benefit us.

If someone lived with pride, for example, to the point that he thought he was *the only one responsible* for everything that life brings him: sight, health and all other gifts, it would not be far from offending the *Grand Master of Life*, the *giant engine*, this great prodigal, the great giver of gifts and benefits.

If we are not able to recognize that we are lucky, *spoiled by life*, in all that it brings, we are almost certain to restrain this *Grand In-charge of all benefits*; precisely because of this attitude of great conceit. That such people don't expect to receive a lot of life! How can it be otherwise!

Would you like to give to an ingrate, to someone who doesn't appreciate your gifts, or don't want to see them?

In the same vein, would you like to meet someone who grumbles all the time? Yet that is what many people do! They wake up growling, cursing events, the temperature. Yet they are often those who can wash with warm water, take a huge lunch, forgetting that much of the world is starving! What did they do special to be born in this part of the world that exudes plenty away from war, far from tsunami?

Others will find the opportunity to be angry, to have a resentment attacks. 'He won't bring it to paradise! He'll have *a dog from my dog*!'As they get excited and they tremble with anger, they don't distill saliva in their mouths, as did the little child, at the idea of chocolate or *Burger King*! Brooding in their hateful thoughts, they will eventually trigger a treacherous chemistry, hidden somewhere in their guts, able to inexorably disturb their inner system.

Can someone have a strong enough health, not to be strongly affected by such poisons? Let us not be surprised to see so many sick people nowadays. Check that they are in their *deep moods*, as suggested by Molière. With what feelings are they inhabited?

As long as my idea remains at the level of my imagination, I can always get to control it or dispose of it. But when it manages to infiltrate me, to live strongly in me, and be part of my being, it can be devastating. When we can feel it, 'sense' it – this word comes from the other word 'sentiment' – so, we can expect a profound reaction.

Imagine someone losing a leg or an eye! '*What does He want from me, from up there?*' he could cry out. And he began to add despair, *non-acceptance, resentment* to this predicament; it would certainly help the devastating internal chemistry to wake up.

Why does it take to lose a limb or sight, to realize how privileged we were before this great misfortune?

If this person was accustomed to appreciate and give thanks for the gifts that life gives him, he would doubtless not have to collect such misfortunes. The gentle chemistry cultivated in a person who feels fulfilled associates more readily to vibrations of the *Infinite*, the Master of life. This person gives more chance to be at *His* tune and be close to his bounty. When you appreciate when you put yourself in the state of someone who is rewarded, who is filled, you hurry the process of gratification. It's a powerful mental cinema, stronger autosuggestion: mentally, you see yourself *already* in possession of what you want. You *saw* it in advance. You *feel... as is*.

Exactly, weren't we taught somewhere that *when we ask any thing to our Heavenly Father, act as if we had already received it!* It's like you said thank you right away to what is coming. You accelerate and become *attracted* to it. This, in my opinion, is the first sense of appreciation and what it can bring.

This process is also similar to that of the Buddhists offering the '*Remembrance!*' In the same way, a Buddhist follower starts in the position of one who *now* remembers what he will succeed in or get *beforehand*! He practices the memory of *already-lived*. It's a different enough phenomenon from the one we know in psychology, because this time it's a *controlled* and *conscious experience*. The other way to succeed also ensures obtaining his desire.

Emmet Fox has also explained the method by the exercise of *Mental Equivalence*. Always the same idea that you maintain in your interior with your thoughts, your feelings, your strong and real beliefs *eventually happen* in your daily life.

All American thinkers and supporters of this way to attract success have experienced it in many ways. The last method they are currently circulating is called '*The Secret*'. A little kept secret, as it's another way to show that our mind has the property of a magnet, attracting the life that is to be obtained, provided you know what you want and you should really be wanting.

We will find this *modus operandi* in most American motivators, along with several followers of *Christian*

Sciences the last century. Just read *Norman Vincent Peale, Joseph Murphy, Zig Ziglar, Napoleon Hill, Clement Stone, Og Mandino* ... and many others.

And what is spectacular through all approaches to life, since we are talking about now is that in fact *it ends up working*!

But don't lose sight of them, that beyond all these ways to attract success, health, abundance, there remains that an approach like the one attributed to Saint Francis, in addition to generating success in our lives, would be the likelihood to eliminate all the small *hurdles* that the Lord of life could encounter, every time we go crazy for doubt, fear, discord in hatred, rancor. Since we would replace that all these irritants, these poisons by noble sentiments, by appreciation!

Always apply the simple method formulated above, one where people learn to be already happy, healthy already, already full of success and happiness, with the result that they always manage to attract all that.

Again, is to apply the positive mental attitude; we act *as if*, we think *as if*, we end up acting *as if*. Some authors even speak of *magic*, with surprising results, unexplained, with such a mental attitude.

LET US CHOOSE...

As much as we can get sick by our thoughts, so we can keep it healthy.

Our frame is fragile.

For example, if I let myself go before you to demonstrate the many ways that exists, biting into a grapefruit, or better in a lemon – *gestures and noises* –

I'd end up making you wince. It would not be the fruit that would make you shudder, because I really don't have any shudders, and you would not see any shudders. It would be the *idea* of a *lemon*, the concept of a *lemon*, with all its *bitter and acidic aspects* that would!

So the same way that the ideas of misfortunes, problems, bad resentments, will you allow your frame to be shaken. Your faces and your thrills are not equally apparent that in front of the imaginary lemon, all dripping; but something like *this chemistry bad blood* may interfere in you, in a *quiet and hypocritical* manner, to gradually mark your deep moods, and then your frame.

I think we should pay attention to this kind of chemistry.

It can make some scientists who don't want to put too much scientific value to this phenomenon, smile, but in fact, we saw countless achievements, as spectacular and as difficult they are to explain.

Why these practitioners do give all the attention and the importance to the disorders and pathologies, rather than covering the health or the maintenance of balance in our frame?

In short, to get there, I know it will of course change our way of thinking and acting. Instead of continuing to follow the course of ease, instead feeding our being with all that is less beautiful, with what's twisted around us, then we will have to decide to change these negative software by more constructive and more positive and above all more *enthusiastic* ones!

Don't forget that the enthusiasm word contains the Greek word *'theos'* (*God*). Whatever our interpretation of God, it should correspond specifically to this great power, which can also be called the *Great Giver of Gifts*.

It's for us, as a sort of invitation to *embark* on the great *Cosmic Plan*: *to be enthusiastic, to be in 'theos'*, in God in some way. Therefore, we agree with the state of mind suggested further when we suggested to appreciate, putting us in tune with the *Generous Head of prosperity*.

Thus, this is the application of the 'funny' way of thinking proposed at the beginning of the book!

Addendum

CAN WE BE HAPPY ALONE?

'*Well!*' Even if it turns round in your head and in your guts, you will not be able to be quite good if you don't succeed in being with others... Remember the motto of Mr. Chantrier: *the art of being well with oneself and with others.*

'With the self first', we said. We talked about it until now. 'And with others,' he added.

I would like to take a quick glance at the latter.

I am sure that everyone realizes that we cannot actually be quite happy alone.

We come from a family, a company, or we live as a couple. In short! We must continually deal with others. It can be easy if we feel attracted, accepted, as it can be more difficult if the missing links that are not present. But the fact remains that we all need to be loved, to be considered, to be significant.

We would then realize that others also have that concern, if not the need.

A good way to get to accept each other is to try to see the good in the other side of the person rather than the less attractive side. In other words, we need to see more of the qualities of the people more than their faults.

If you see only their weaknesses, you can never find the friendly. Unfortunately, much importance is given to what is wrong with someone. In *interviews*, we hear too often this kind of question, 'What is your biggest flaw?' One should think that every time we mention a fault, it's believed to be a fault, and we give importance to something unwanted, negative. There is no progress in the construction of a person by putting the *focus* on what is wrong.

Whereas if they spoke as one would think esteem, one would think of admiration.

Although the qualities we stress aren't to the maximum, at least we start on the road to become better.

All this could start in our surroundings, with friends, with family especially.

My mother? She has no qualities!' *Nope!* A mother who had a bunch of kids to bring up, to *scold* as Molière said, surely has no qualities!

Not easy to recognize them! But when you get used to *look* on the bright side of people, we forget more easily what is wrong, what gets on our *nerves!* Even if people don't always have the art of attracting sympathy, you still have to admit that they necessarily hold some values!

Maybe the sense of importance, which is deeply embedded in each of us, keeps us very often from giving others the look and consideration they deserve, too concerned as we are by this need to be the king or queen of the place!

Is that by giving too much importance to us, that we happen to not wanting to give the same importance to others? Especially when we *buttered them up?* If one puts too much, instead of attracting sympathy, he could end up upsetting them. They too, have this need to be significant; we must remember. Trying to show them that we have '*it, the x-factor,*' it's almost guaranteed to be at fault somewhere. And often people will be tempted to want to diminish us.

Anyone can remember easily the one who managed to make a bad first impression.

'*Him, over there...*'

There is just a saying that reminds us of that idea: *It's already wrong to have been too right!*

Man is made so.

Epilogue

Finally, much as I can turn the ways of living life, from all angles, I realize that we cannot escape the real 'things'!

That one makes his own path, which goes through a lot of experiments, and we should eventually arrive at the same conclusion: there can be *multiple* truths when it comes to live his life. There is *one*, in fact *the one* put forward by most of the major philosophers and thinkers; that nearly all workers of Human Sciences offer us everywhere; also the one I told you about in this little book, that of thinking positively, *that* of Believing!

To believe means to *believe in life, believe in yourself!* The assessment later became a sort of spontaneous manifestation of this belief, this faith in life!

In short! All the beautiful *game plan* that is being proposed and always wants us to sink our teeth sooner into this wonderful life has always been based on that faith in life, *faith* in all, indeed!

Thus, for more than thirty years, I have supported this kind of thinking in my activity rooms. For over thirty years I heard myself tell it to *me*.

Today, twenty years later, I'm still steeped in this 'funny' way of thinking. I cannot say precisely where I get all my beliefs about the *rules of life*. Is it the fruit of the way I was educated? Is it the fruit of my studies? Is it from the positive messages conveyed during my years of work? In short, it is from all these sources, at the same time.

After spending a lifetime finding solutions to the difficulties encountered by humans, it's normal to not necessarily doubt the positive in life, and splendor.

In general, we can always dip any teaching of anything that emanates a life of learning, and we can learn from experiences of others; but when it was really lived oneself, one ends up quite grasping them well. A life situation works better than a speech.

So, that is why *'je m'ébaudis'!*

This means something like : '*I am very happy*' to see that there are still experiences where one doesn't just say things, but where one allows followers to practice!

I hesitated a long time before I got in the unveiling of this message. I finally said that it could help those who may never be able to pay for group experiments where you can discover this wonderful lifestyle.

Why not a second epilogue?

Human beings often fear success here. It has been used to deal with a system where *talented* people are often put aside. In school, if you finish your work too quickly, we'll send you sometimes to waste your time in the hallway waiting for those who are slower to finish. On the other hand, several specialists will take care of you if you have major problems.

Today's teachers waste their energies to deal mostly with the *laggards, those characters,* sacrificing other students full of talent.

It's also made that way in society. Let us remember this striking example of it a few years ago, when the *Canadian Hockey Club* had become very strong, almost unbeatable. We then found a way to prevent it from being even better, forcing it to stop fishing for good players.

It's quite easy to reach the efficiency of a team by lowering their performance, rather than trying to become as good as it can be! We prefer leveling clubs down , sacrificing excellence!

Our education invites us to shun the elite, to snub success. We will have to fight *constantly* to counteract this spirit of ease.

I always think of *Jonathan Livingstone 'The Seagull'* by Richard Bach. Jonathan was despised by his peers because he wanted to fly *ever higher*, rather than stick to pecking around restaurants.

So we will have to deal with a lax society where everything must be easy, inconsequential. We will deal with this kind of society where the mass must be sovereign. People will not want to rely on themselves; they will wait for a *'good'* government. Always wanting to rely on others, rather than on themselves, people will find more space to criticize thereafter.

This proposed way, to see life with confidence, will always be something unusual to too many people. Some will continue to seek answers in dummy values, in the material; while everything has to happen more in the attitude, in the state of mind, in the mind of each.

This isn't because a man is at the top of the social scale that he suddenly develops a winning attitude and becomes good. It's because he was good and had the right attitude at the start, he came up the steps of the social hierarchy and success.

THE KILLER QUESTION...

The killer question is: 'To be happy, must you always rely on others? Or should you instead rely on yourself?'

You can guess my answer, of course. You also know the way that I prefer to get there: the assiduous practice of good mental attitude and continuous positive thinking.

With perseverance, we will meet the challenge. This will be the guarantee for everyone to be proud of themselves.

ANDRÉ DAIGLE

www.ingramcontent.com/pod-product-compliance
Lightning Source LLC
Chambersburg PA
CBHW072159100426
42738CB00011BA/2472